FOR ORGANS, PIANOS & ELECTRONIC KEYBOARDS

E-Z PLAY® TODAY

26

Cover photo: Jerry Schatzberg / Trunk Archive

ISBN 978-1-61780-772-5

Music Sales America

Exclusively Distributed By

Hal•Leonard®
CORPORATION

7777 W. Bluemound Rd. P.O. Box 13819 Milwaukee, WI 53213

E-Z Play® Today Music Notation © 1975 by HAL LEONARD CORPORATION
E-Z PLAY and EASY ELECTRONIC KEYBOARD MUSIC are registered trademarks of HAL LEONARD CORPORATION.

Visit Hal Leonard Online at
**www.halleonard.com**

# All Along the Watchtower

Registration 4
Rhythm: Rock

Words and Music by
Bob Dylan

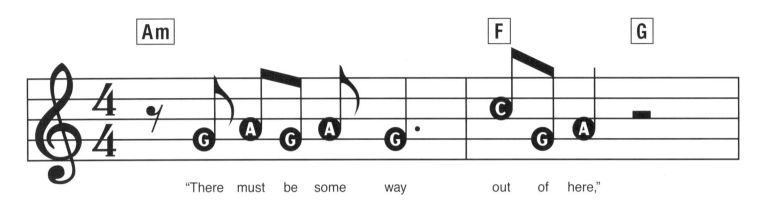

"There must be some way out of here,"

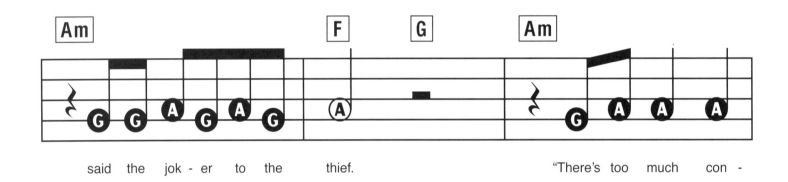

said the jok-er to the thief. "There's too much con-

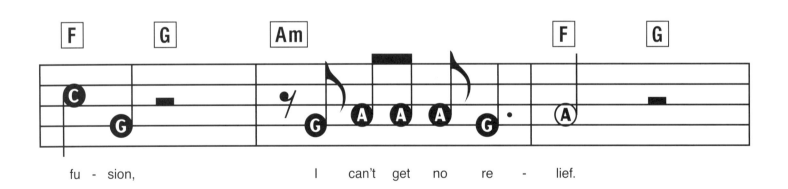

fu - sion, I can't get no re - lief.

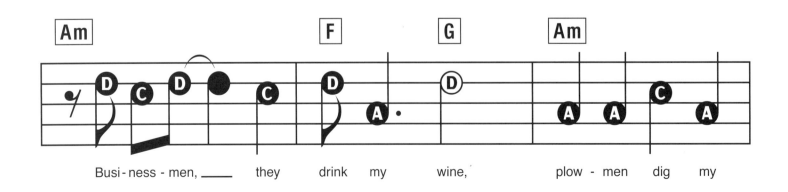

Busi-ness-men, _____ they drink my wine, plow-men dig my

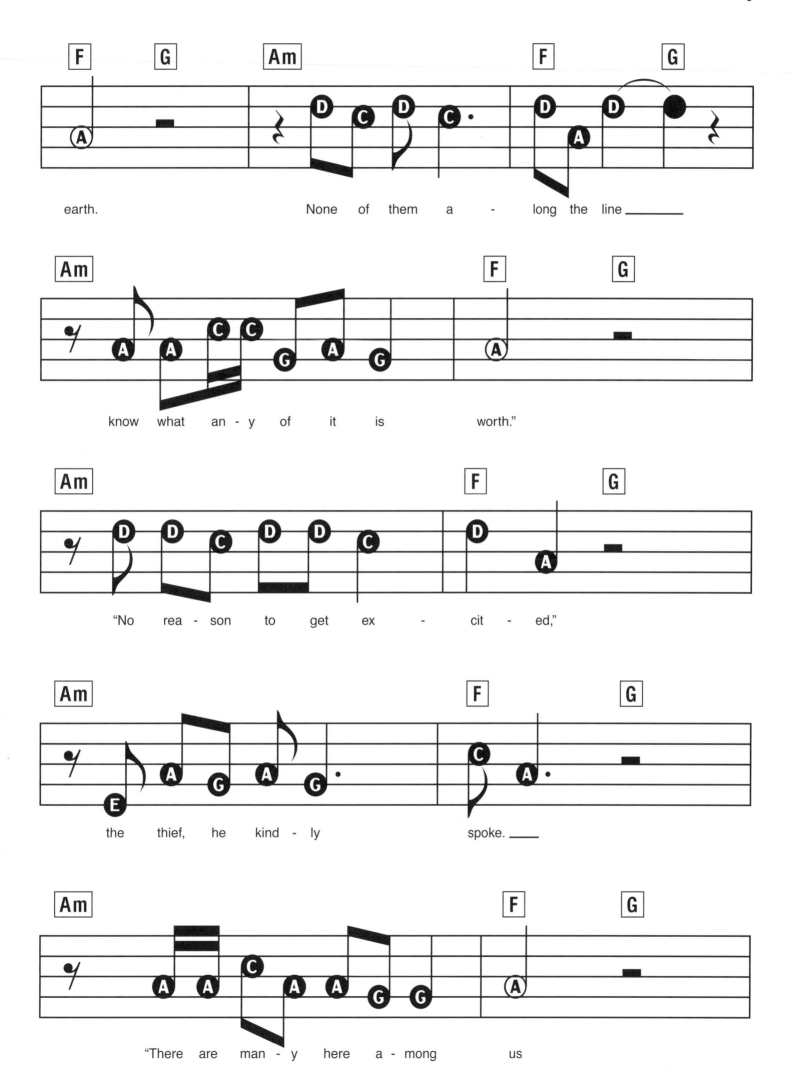

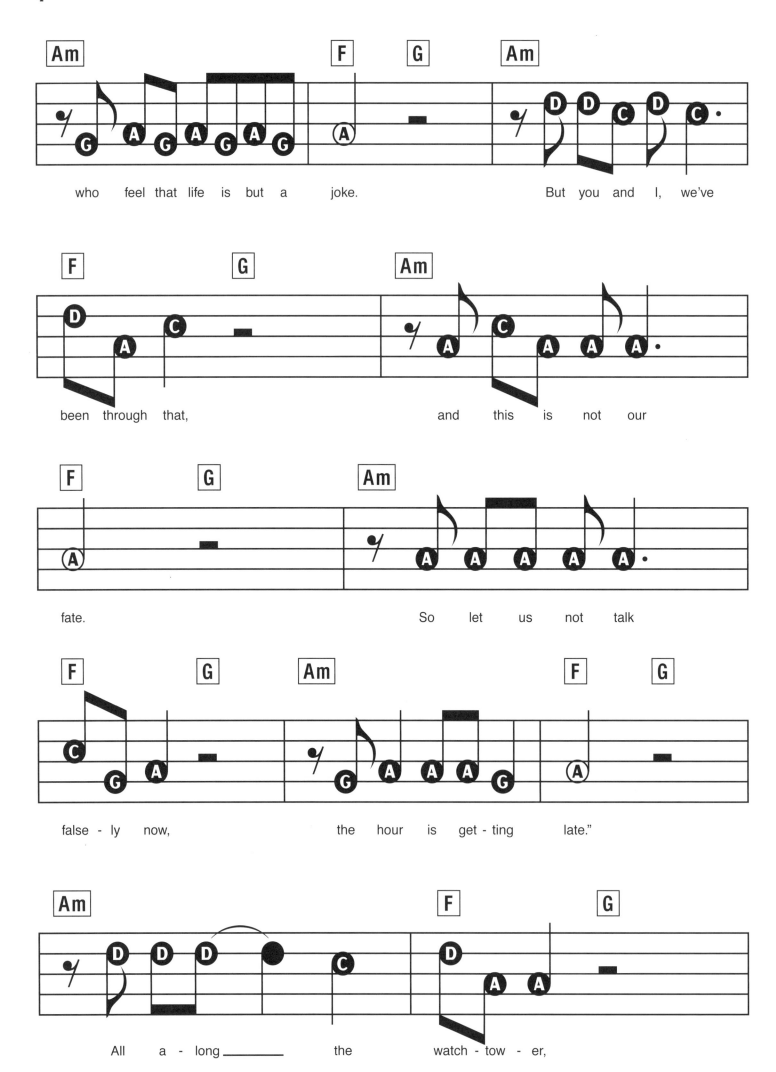

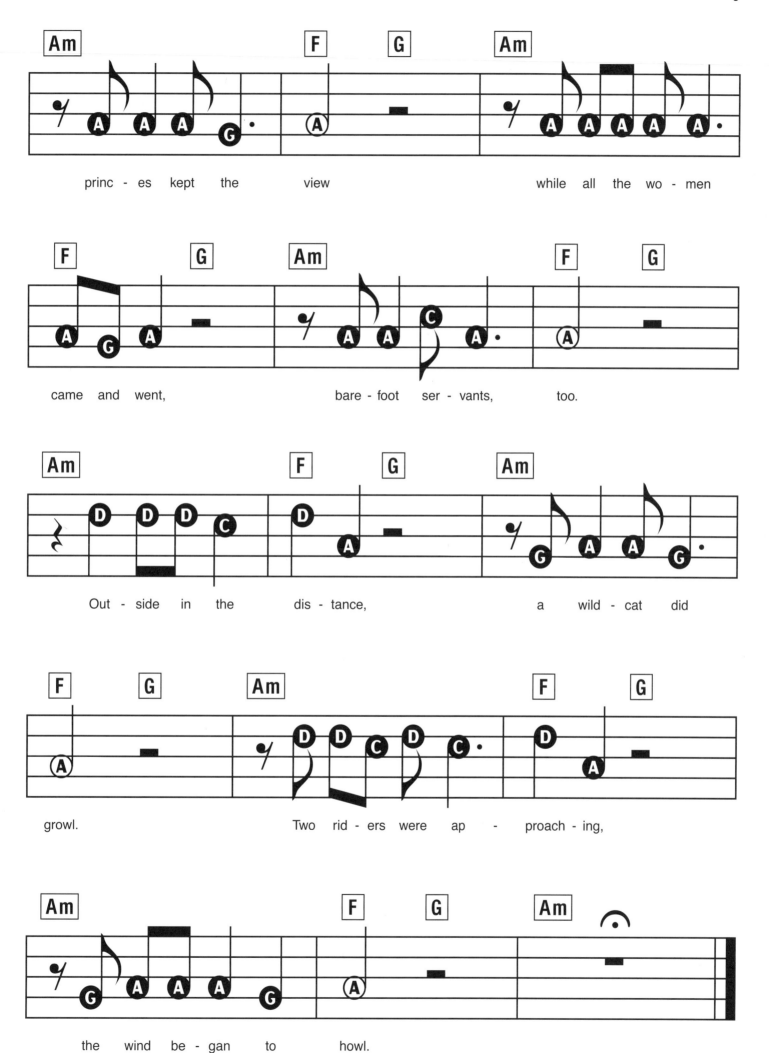

# Blowin' in the Wind

Registration 4
Rhythm: Ballad or Fox Trot

Words and Music by
Bob Dylan

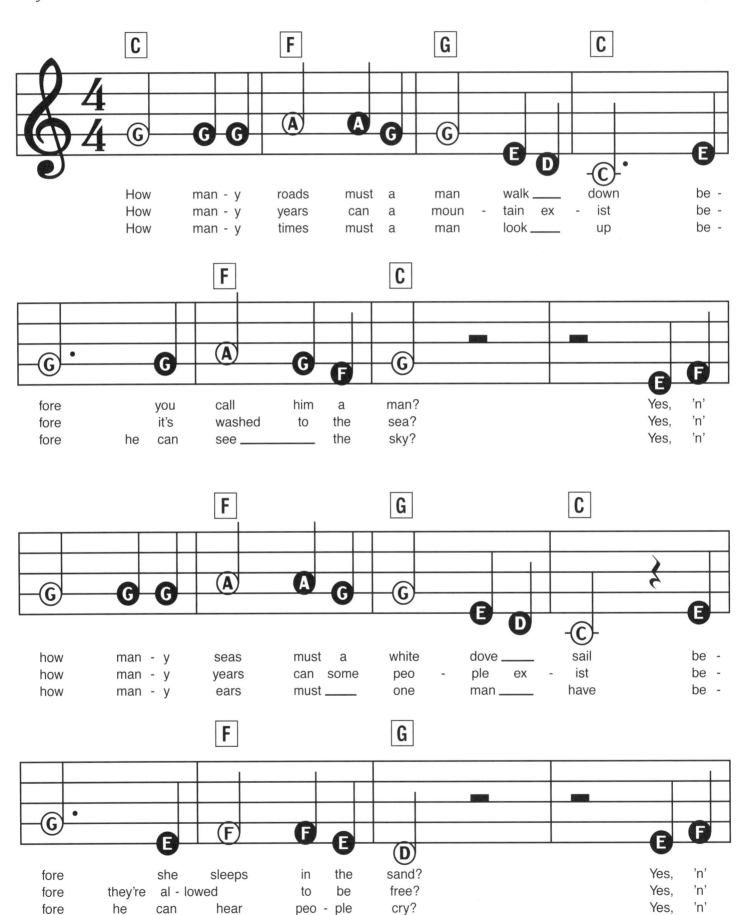

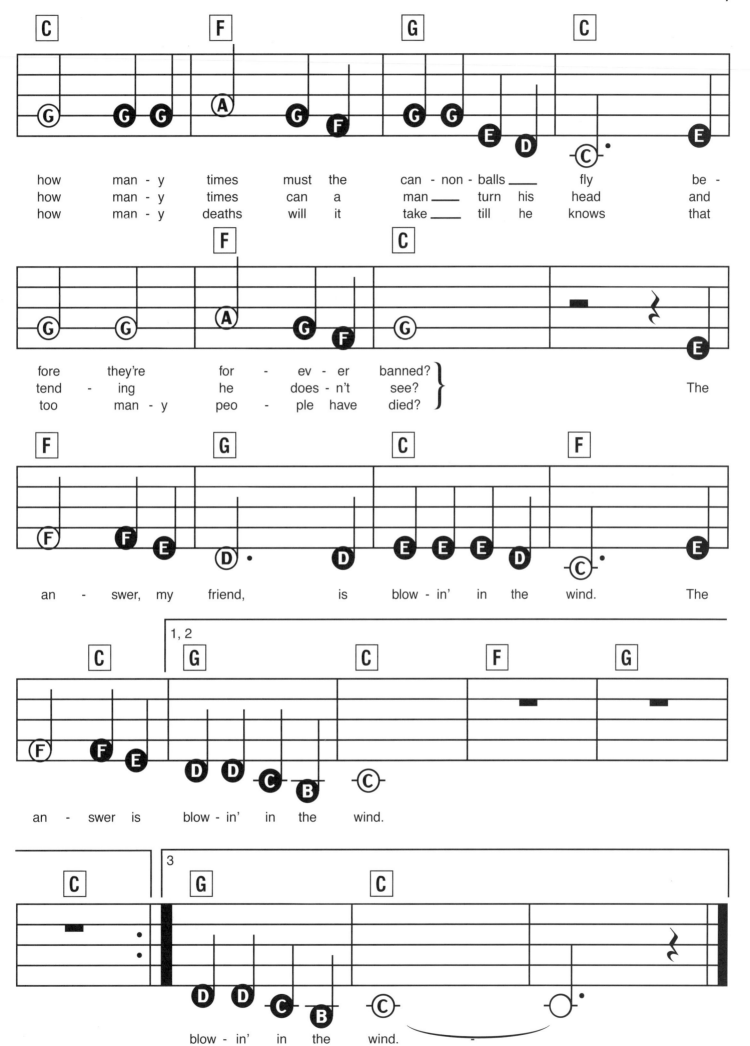

# Forever Young

Registration 4
Rhythm: 8-Beat or Rock

Words and Music by
Bob Dylan

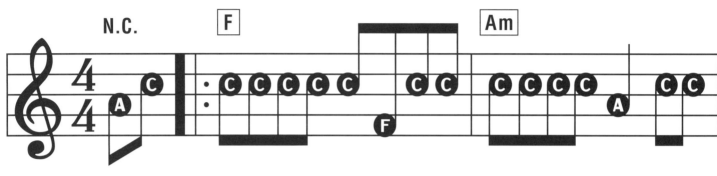

May God bless and keep you al - ways. May your wish - es all come true. May you
grow up to be right-eous. May you grow up to be true. May you

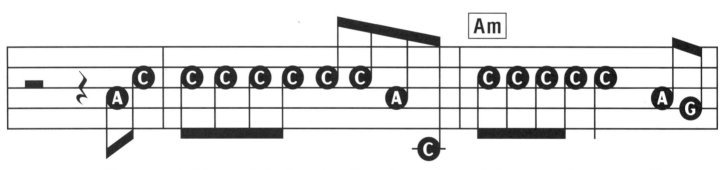

al - ways do for oth - ers and let oth - ers do for you.
al - ways know the truth and see the lights sur - round - ing you.

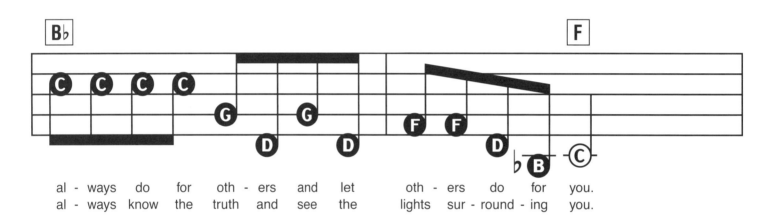

May you build a lad - der to the stars, and climb on ev - 'ry rung. May you
May you al - ways be cou - ra - geous, stand up - right and be ___ strong. May you

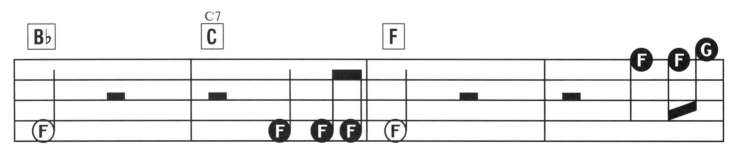

stay for - ev - er young. For - ev - er
stay for - ev - er young. For - ev - er

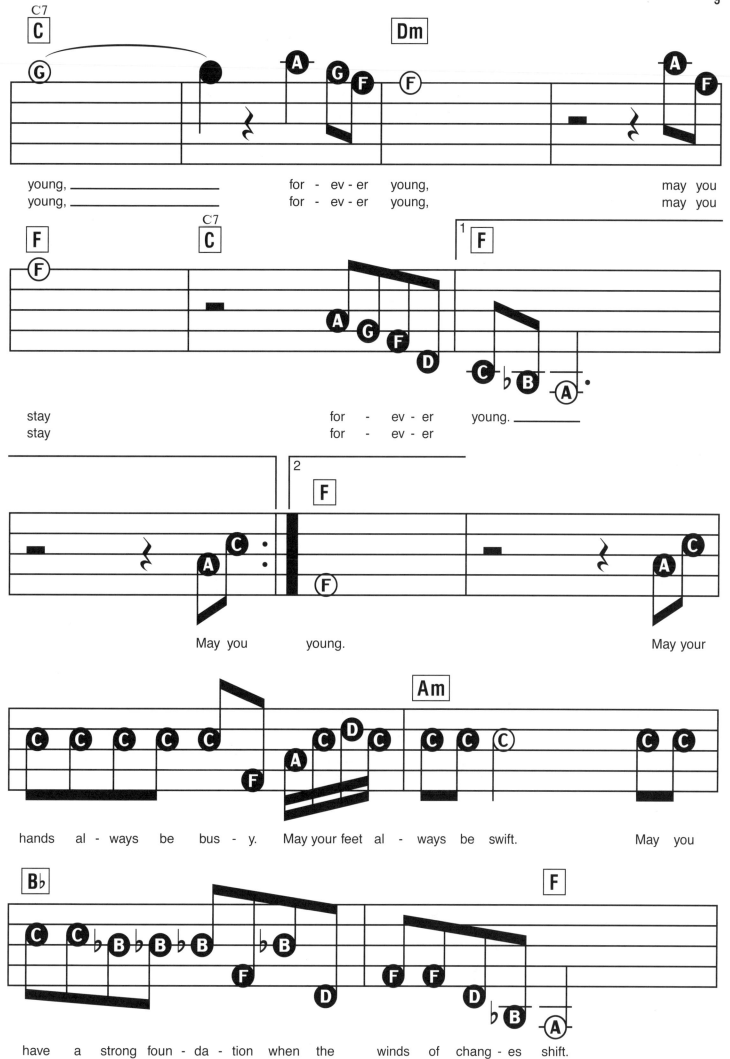

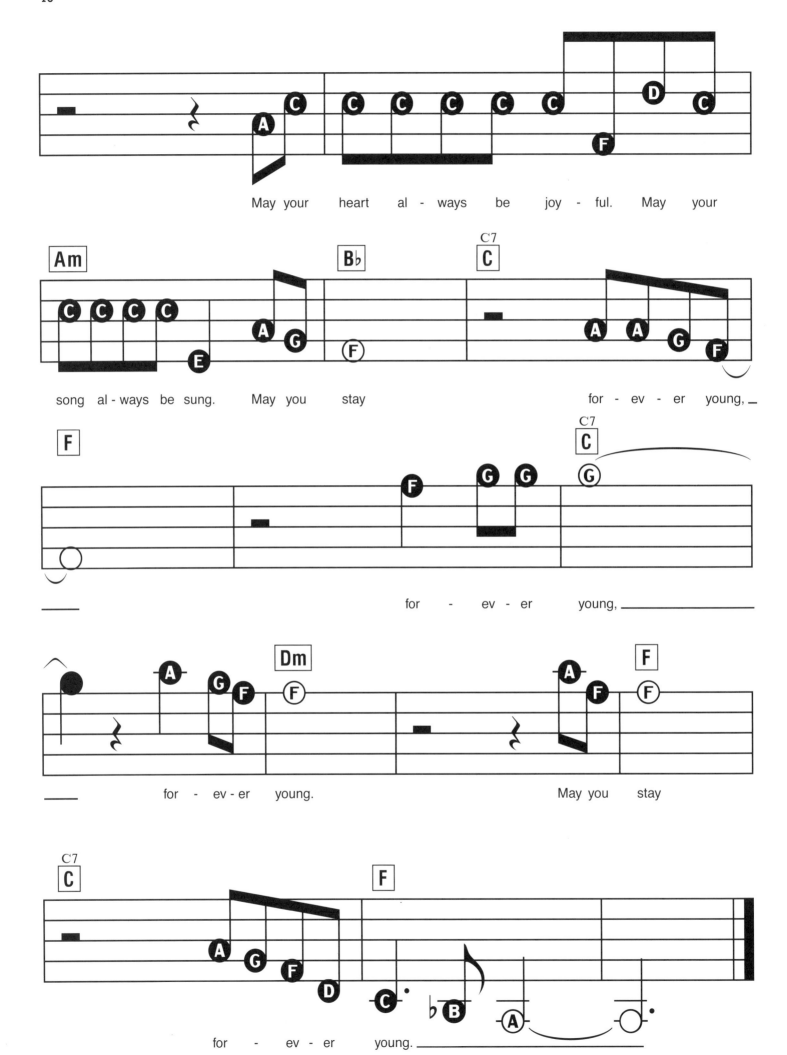

# It Ain't Me Babe

Registration 4
Rhythm: Country Pop or Fox Trot

Words and Music by
Bob Dylan

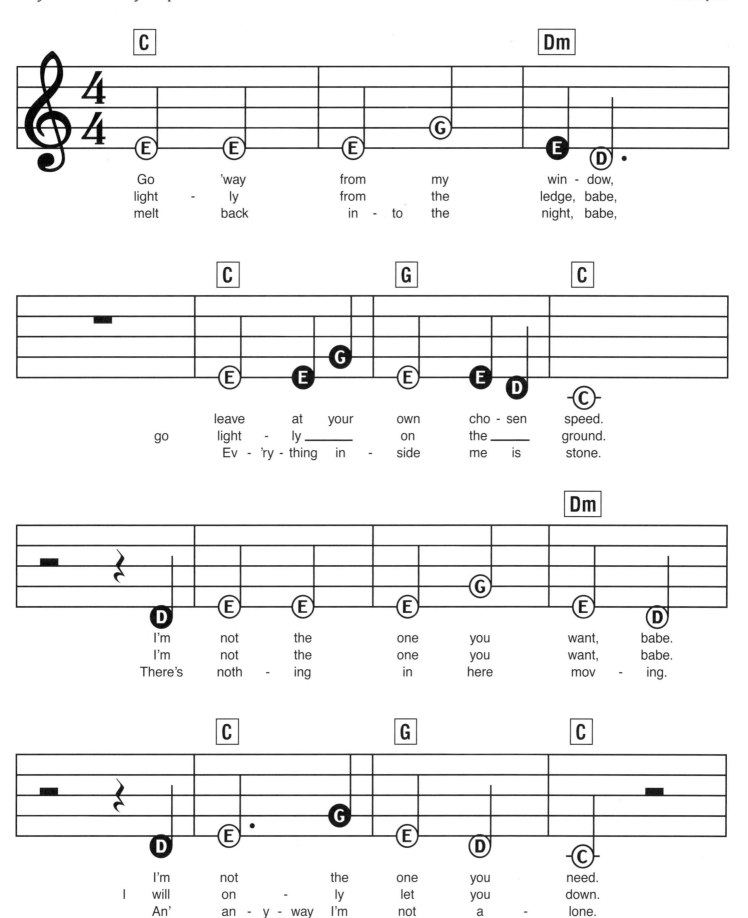

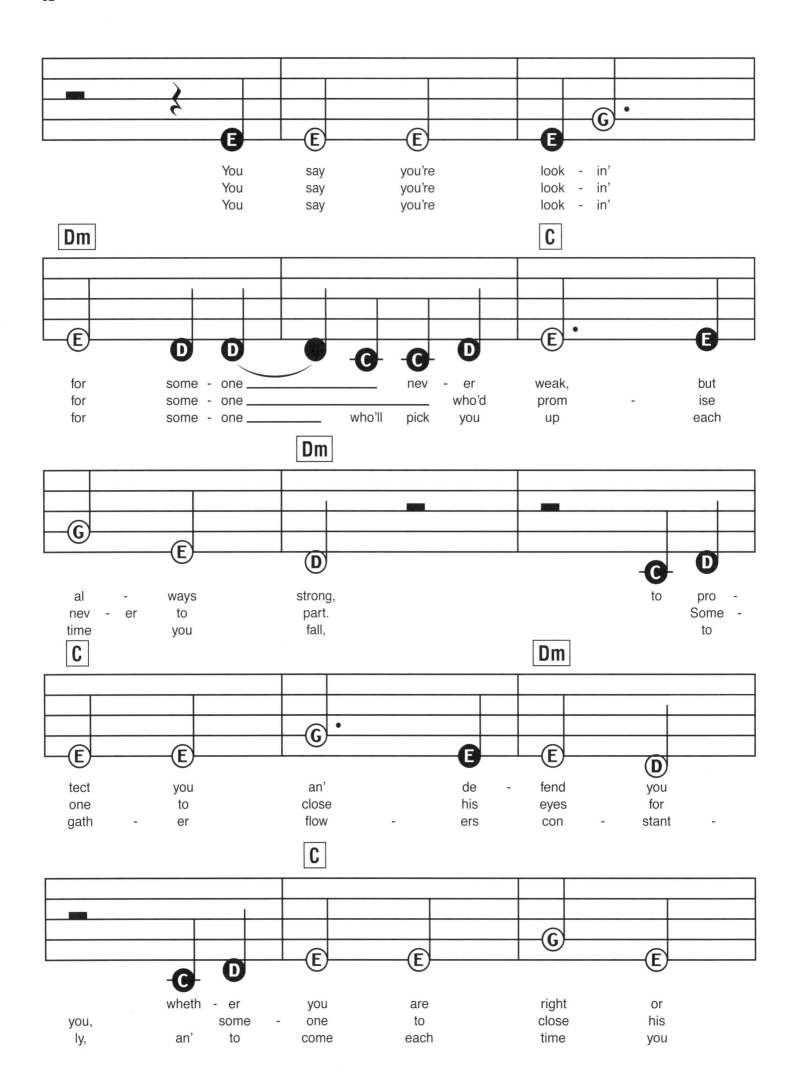

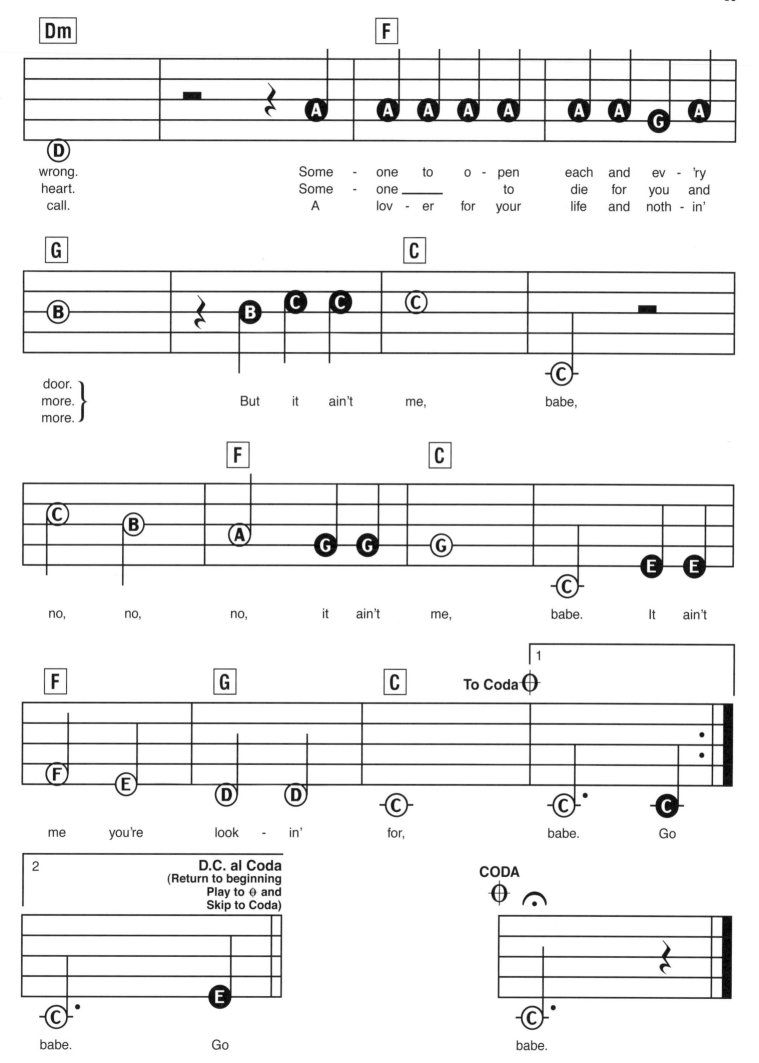

# Hurricane

Registration 4
Rhythm: 8-Beat or Rock

Words and Music by Bob Dylan
and Jacques Levy

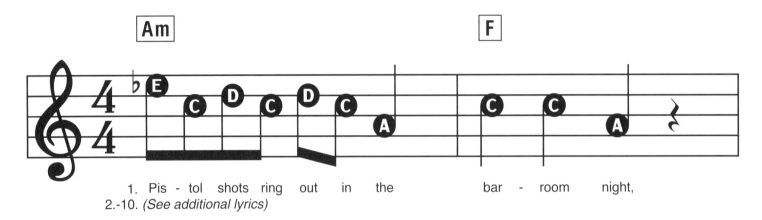

1. Pis - tol shots ring out in the bar - room night,
2.-10. *(See additional lyrics)*

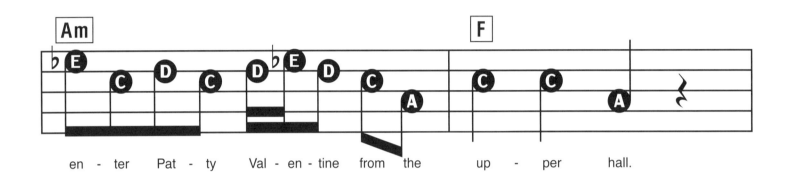

en - ter Pat - ty Val - en - tine from the up - per hall.

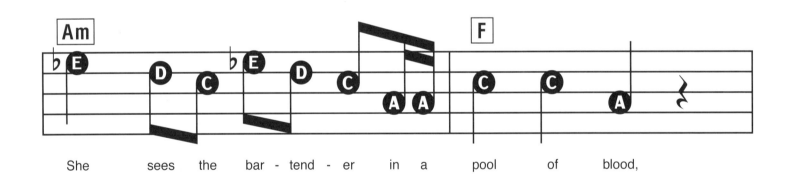

She sees the bar - tend - er in a pool of blood,

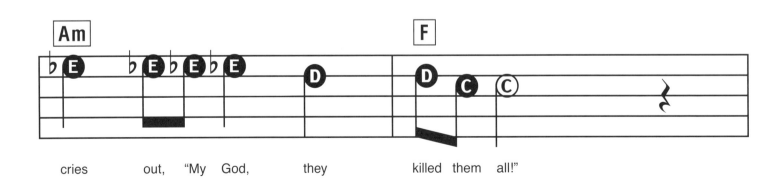

cries out, "My God, they killed them all!"

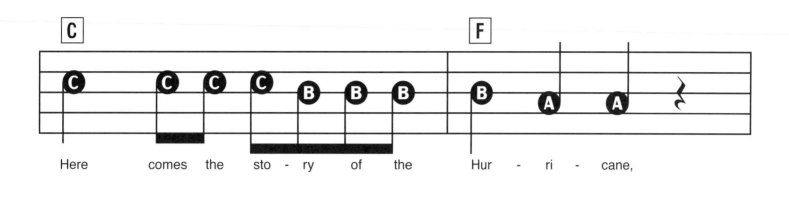

Here comes the story of the Hur - ri - cane,

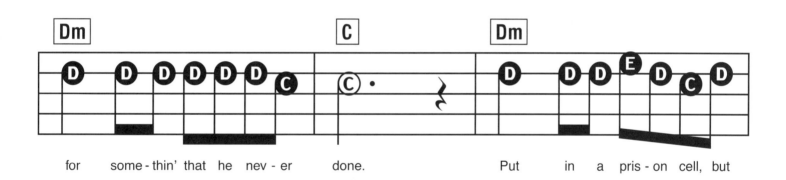

the man the au - thor - i - ties came to blame

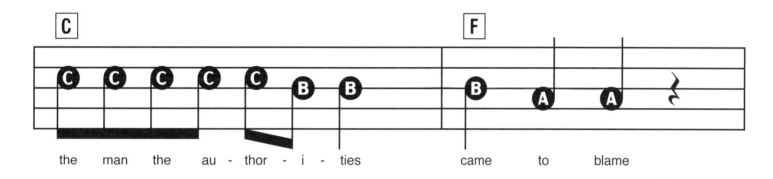

for some - thin' that he nev - er done. Put in a pris - on cell, but

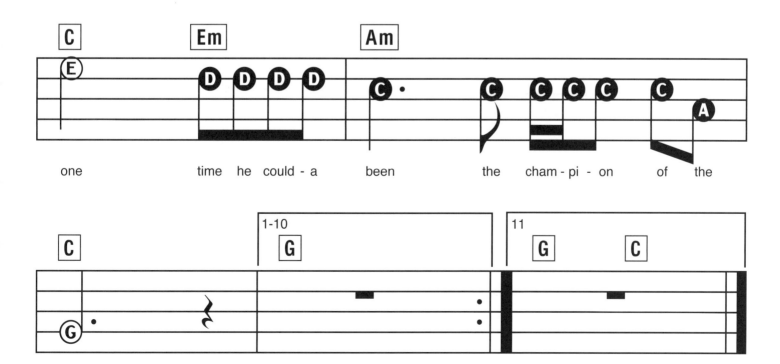

one time he could - a been the cham - pi - on of the

world.

*Additional Lyrics*

2. Three bodies lyin' there does Patty see
   And another man named Bello, movin' around mysteriously
   "I didn't do it," he says, and he throws up his hands
   "I was only robbin' the register, I hope you understand
   I saw them leavin'," he says, and he stops
   "One of us had better call up the cops"
   And so Patty calls the cops
   And they arrive on the scene with their red lights flashin'
   In the hot New Jersey night

3. Meanwhile, far away in another part of town
   Rubin Carter and a couple of friends are drivin' around
   Number one contender for the middlewieght crown
   Had no idea what kinda shit was about to go down
   When a cop pulled him over to the side of the road
   Just like the time before and the time before that
   In Paterson that's just the way things go
   If you're black you might as well not show up on the street
   'Less you wanta draw the heat

4. Alfred Bello had a partner and he had a rap for the cops
   Him and Arthur Dexter Bradley were just out prowlin' around
   He said, "I saw two men runnin' out, they looked like middleweights
   They jumped into a white car with out-of-state plates"
   And Miss Patty Valentine just nodded her head
   Cop said, "Wait a minute boys, this one's not dead"
   So they took him to the infirmary
   And though this man could hardly see
   They told him that he could identify the guilty men

5. Four in the mornin' and they haul Rubin in
   Take him to the hospital and they bring him upstairs
   The wounded man looks up through his one dyin' eye
   Says, "Wha'd you bring him in here for? He ain't the guy!"
   Yes, here's the story of the Hurricane
   The man the authorities came to blame
   For somethin' that he never done
   Put in a prison cell, but one time he could-a been
   The champion of the world

6. Four months later, the ghettos are in flame
   Rubin's in South America, fightin' for his name
   While Arthur Dexter Bradley's still in the robbery game
   And the cops are puttin' the screws to him, lookin' for somebody to blame
   "Remember that murder that happened in a bar?"
   "Remember you said you saw the getaway car?"
   "You think you'd like to play ball with the law?"
   "Think it mighta been that fighter that you saw runnin' that night?"
   "Don't forget that you are white"

7. Arthur Dexter Bradley said, "I'm really not sure"
   Cops said, "A poor boy like you could use a break
   We got you for the motel job and we're talkin' to your friend Bello
   Now you don't wanta have to go back to jail, be a nice fellow
   You'll be doin' society a favor
   That sonofabitch is brave and gettin' braver
   We want to put his ass in stir
   We want to pin this triple murder on him
   He ain't no Gentleman Jim"

8. Rubin could take a man out with just one punch
   But he never did like to talk about it all that much
   It's my work, he'd say, and I do it for pay
   And when it's over I'd just as soon go on my way
   Up to some paradise
   Where the trout streams flow and the air is nice
   And ride a horse along a trail
   But then they took him to the jailhouse
   Where they try to turn a man into a mouse

9. All of Rubin's cards were marked in advance
   The trial was a pig-circus, he never had a chance
   The judge made Rubin's witnesses drunkards from the slums
   To the white folks who watched he was a revolutionary bum
   And to the black folks he was just a crazy nigger
   No one doubted that he pulled the trigger
   And though they could not produce the gun
   The D.A. said he was the one who did the deed
   And the all-white jury agreed

10. Rubin Carter was falsely tried
    The crime was murder "one," guess who testified?
    Bello and Bradley and they both baldly lied
    And the newspapers, they all went along for the ride
    How can the life of such a man
    Be in the palm of some fool's hand?
    To see him obviously framed
    Couldn't help but make me feel ashamed to live in a land
    Where justice is a game

11. Now all the criminals in their coats and their ties
    Are free to drink martinis and watch the sun rise
    While Rubin sits like Buddha in a ten-foot cell
    An innocent man in a living hell
    That's the story of the Hurricane
    But it won't be over till they clear his name
    And give him back the time he's done
    Put in a prison cell, but one time he could-a been
    The champion of the world

# Just Like a Woman

Registration 4
Rhythm: Country Rock or Rock

Words and Music by
Bob Dylan

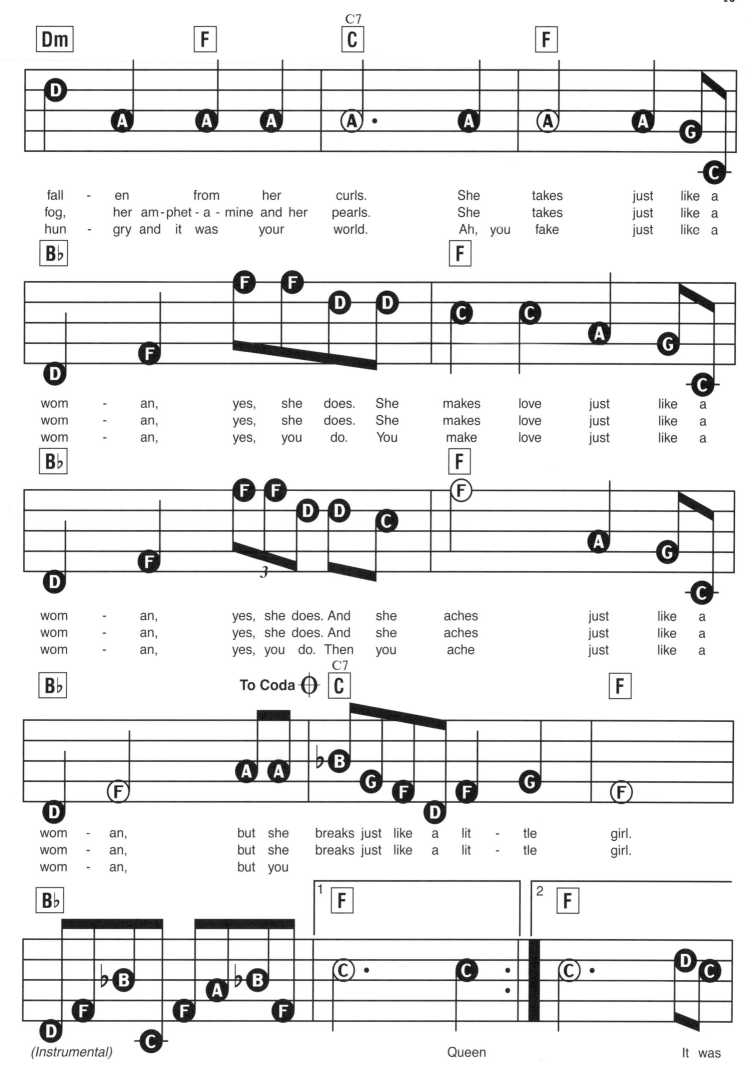

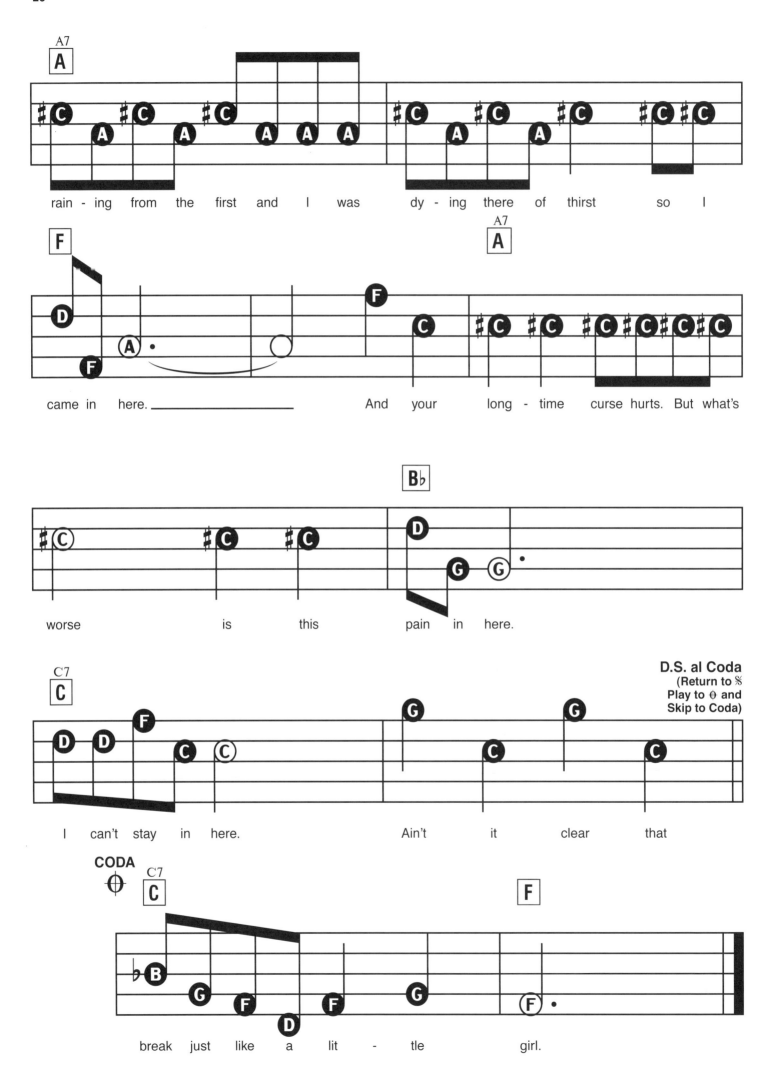

# Lay Lady Lay

Registration 7
Rhythm: 8-Beat or Rock

Words and Music by
Bob Dylan

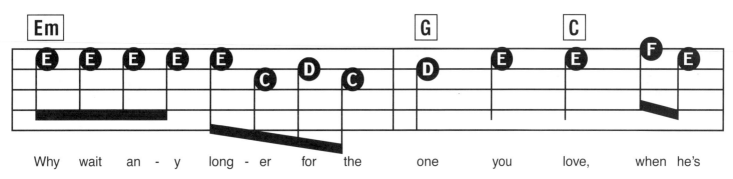

Why wait an - y long - er for the one you love, when he's

**D.C. al Coda**
(Return to beginning
Play to ⊕ and
Skip to Coda)

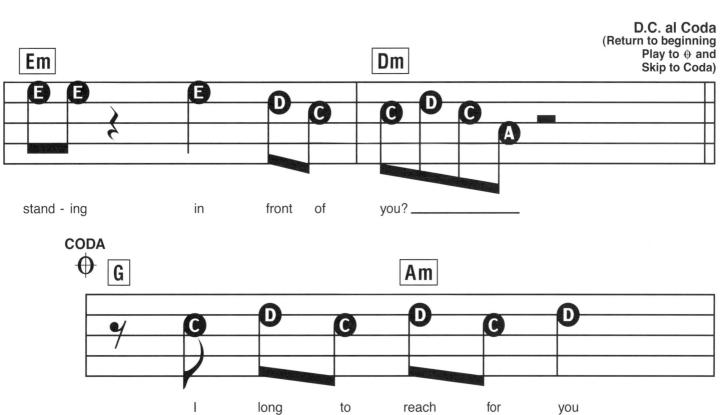

stand - ing in front of you? _____

**CODA**

I long to reach for you

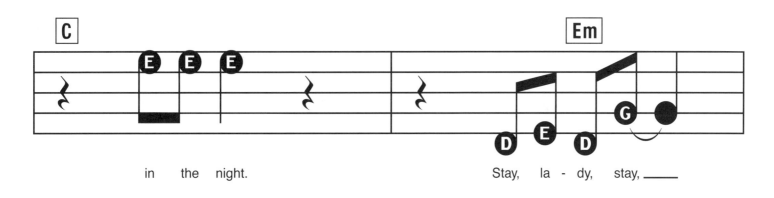

in the night. Stay, la - dy, stay, ____

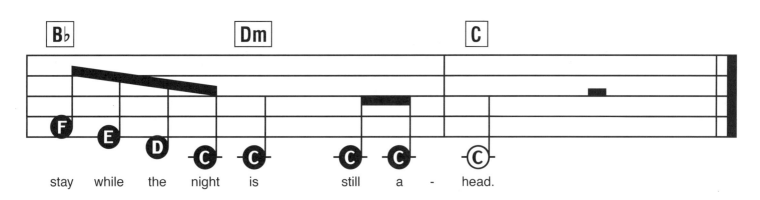

stay while the night is still a - head.

# Knockin' on Heaven's Door

Registration 4
Rhythm: 8-Beat or Rock

Words and Music by
Bob Dylan

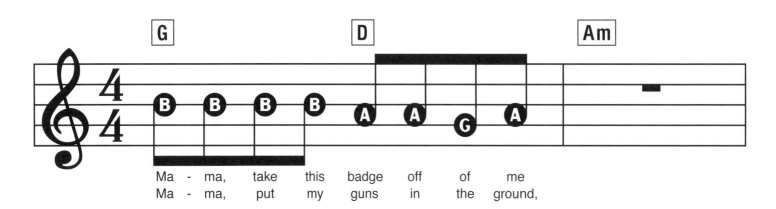

Ma - ma, take this badge off of me
Ma - ma, put my guns in the ground,

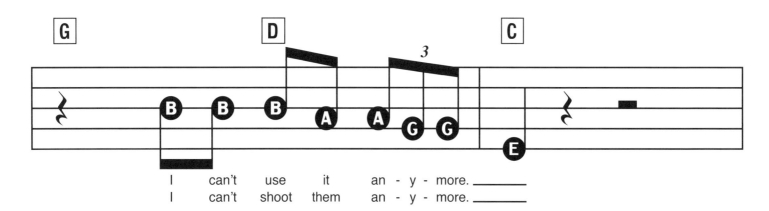

I can't use it an - y - more. _____
I can't shoot them an - y - more. _____

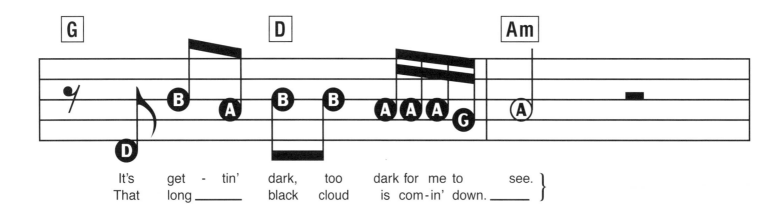

It's get - tin' dark, too dark for me to see. }
That long _____ black cloud is com - in' down. _____ }

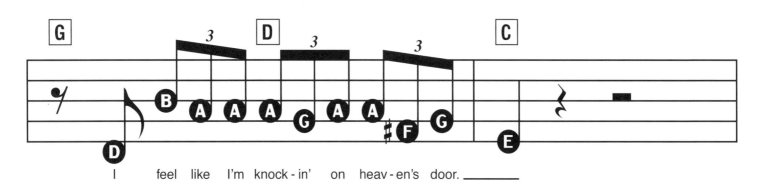

I feel like I'm knock - in' on heav - en's door. _____

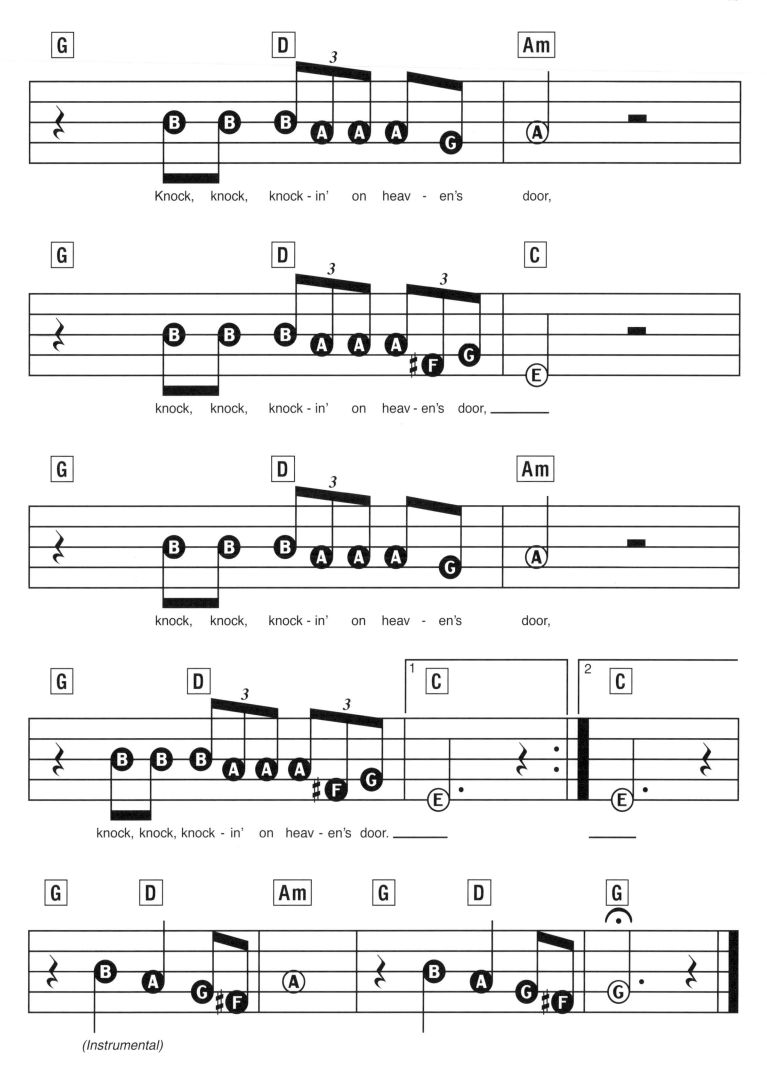

# Like a Rolling Stone

Registration 8
Rhythm: 8-Beat or Rock

Words and Music by
Bob Dylan

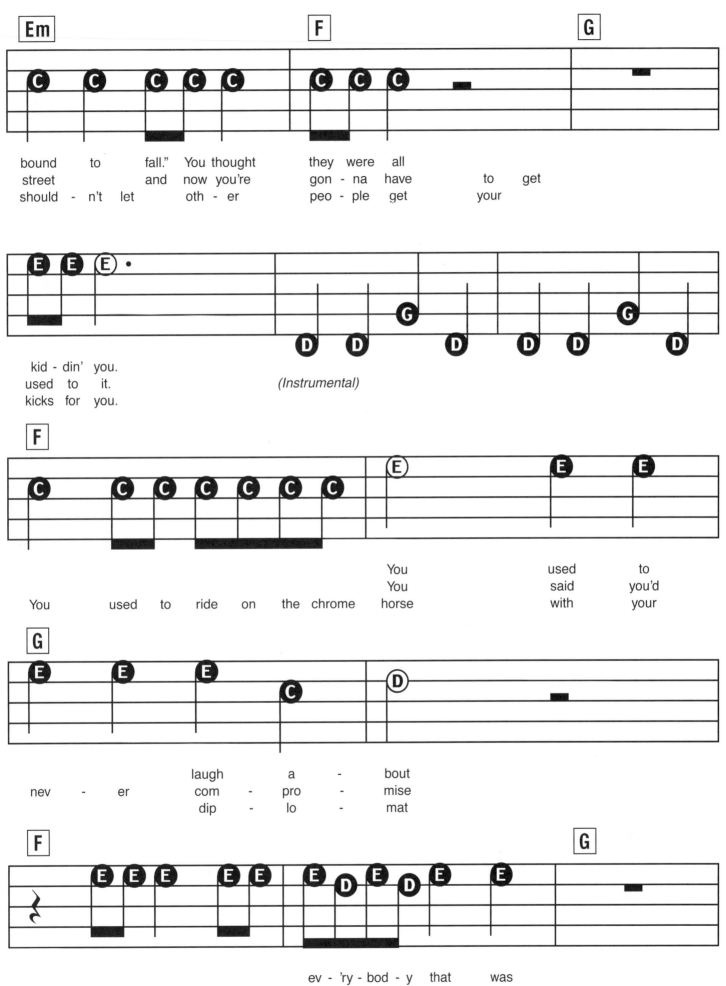

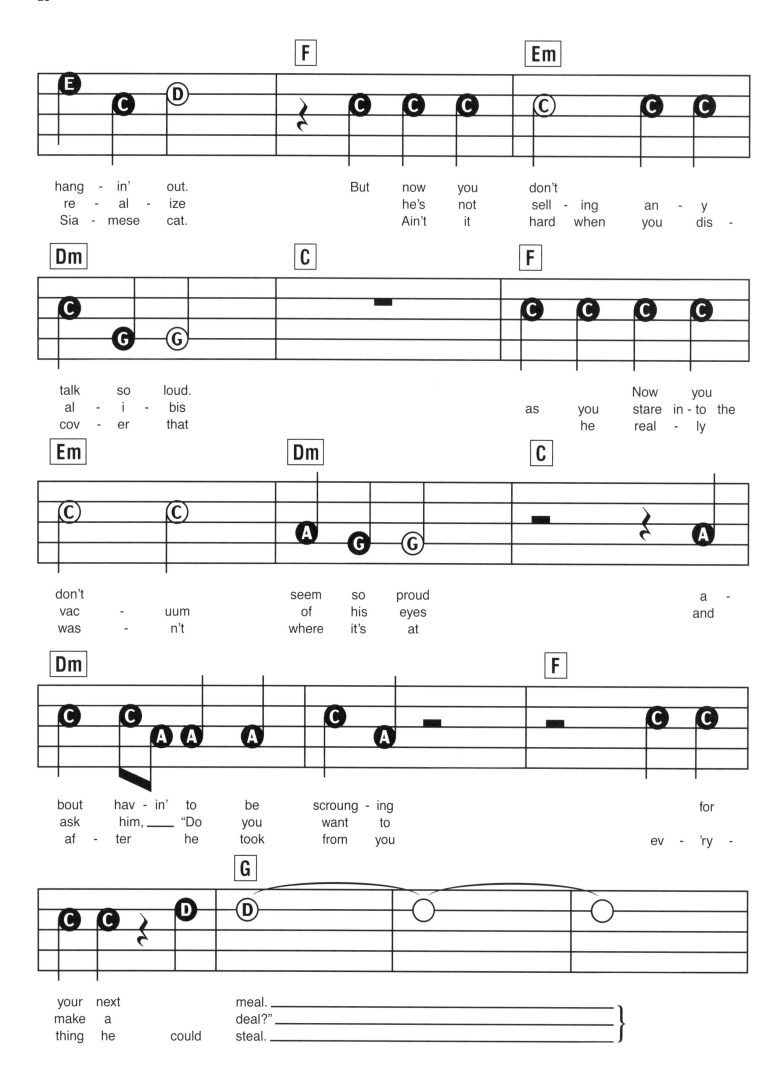

**Chorus**

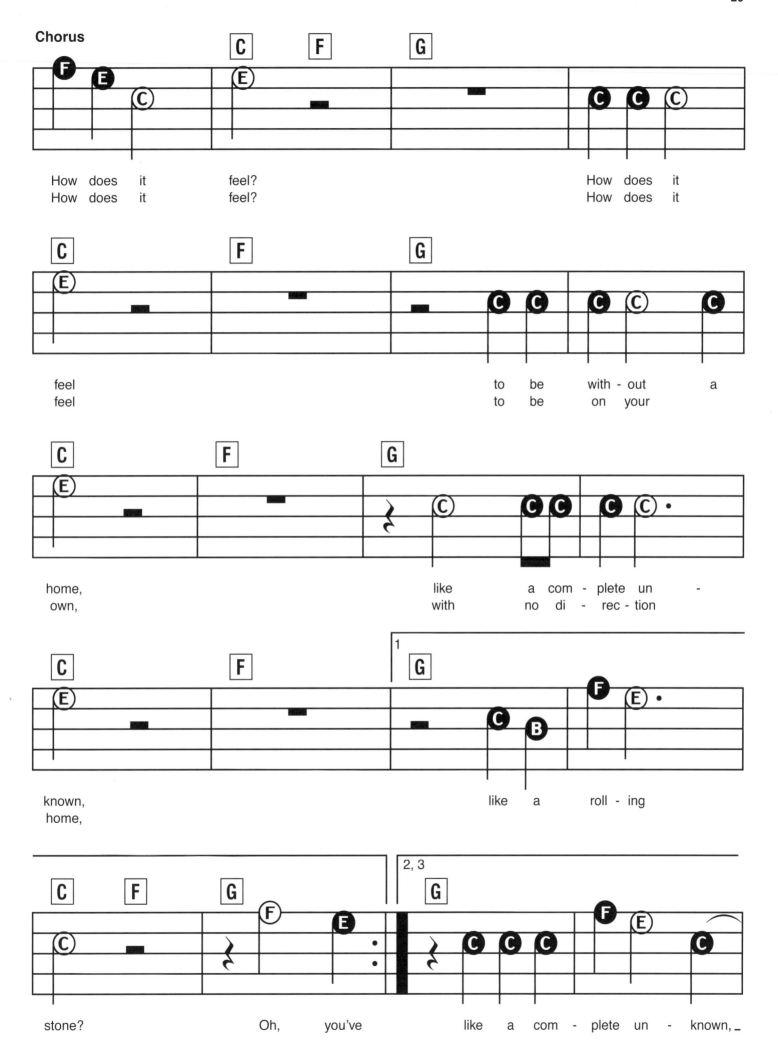

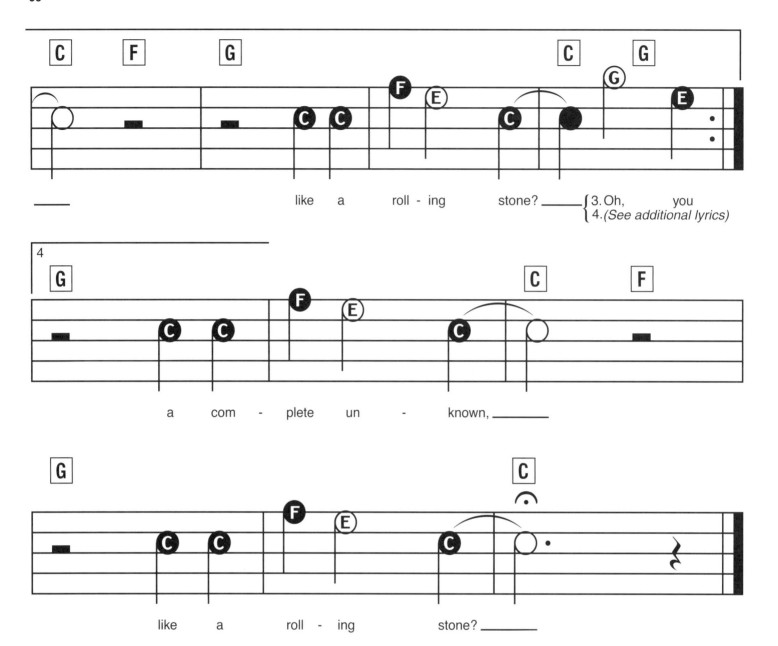

like a roll - ing stone? _____ { 3. Oh, you
{ 4. *(See additional lyrics)*

a com - plete un - known, _____

like a roll - ing stone? _____

*Additional Lyrics*

4. Princess on the steeple and all the pretty people
They're all drinkin', thinkin' that they got it made.
Exchanging all kinds of precious gifts and things,
But you'd better lift your diamond ring,
You'd better pawn it, babe.
You used to be so amused
At Napoleon in rags and the language that he used.
Go to him now, he calls you, you can't refuse.
When you got nothing, you got nothing to lose.
You're invisible now, you got no secrets to conceal.
*Chorus*

# Mr. Tambourine Man

Registration 8
Rhythm: Rock

Words and Music by
Bob Dylan

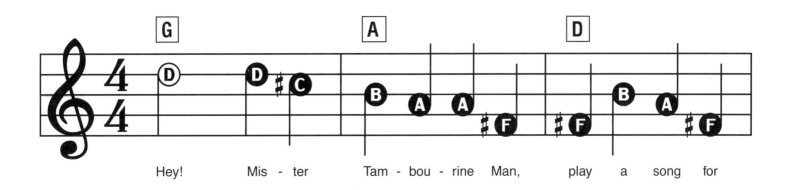

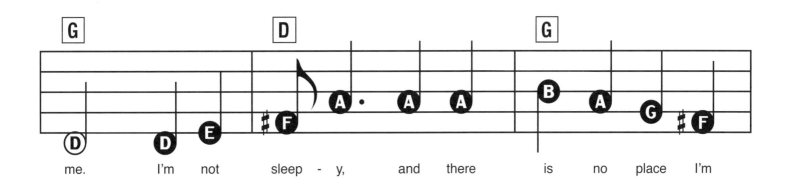

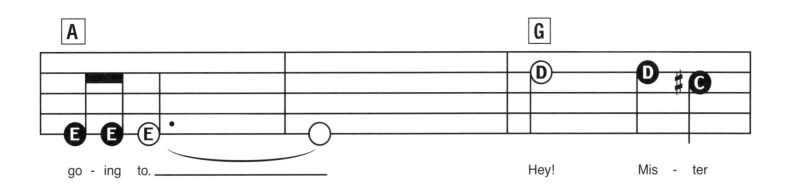

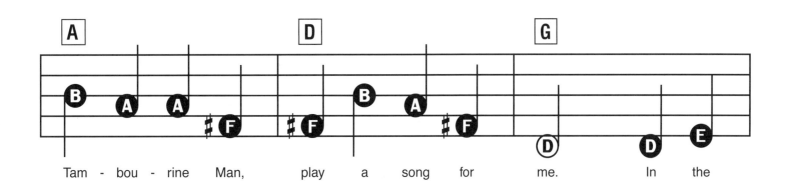

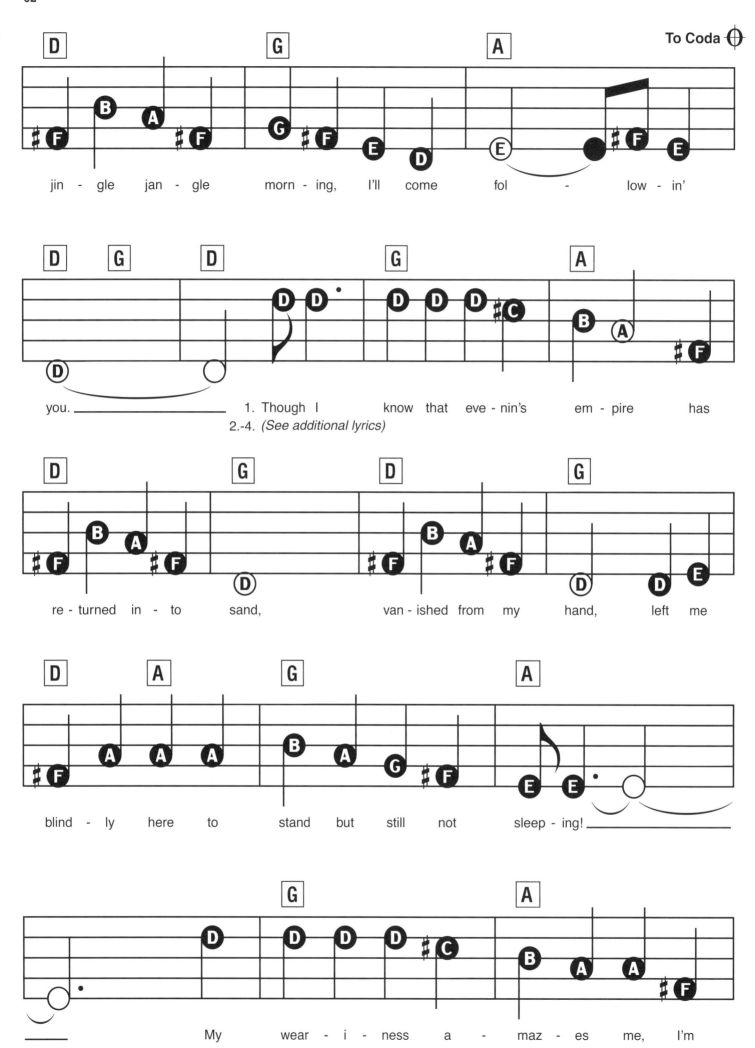

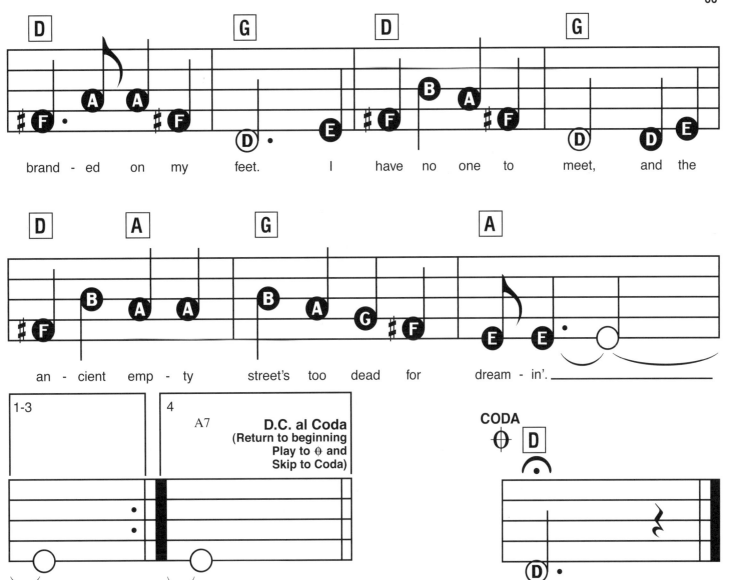

brand - ed on my feet. I have no one to meet, and the

an - cient emp - ty street's too dead for dream - in'. _____

**1-3**

**4**
A7
**D.C. al Coda**
(Return to beginning
Play to ⊕ and
Skip to Coda)

**CODA**
**D**

you.

*Additional Lyrics*

2. Take me on a trip upon your magic swirlin' ship
   My senses have been stripped, my hands can't feel to grip
   My toes too numb to step,
   Wait only for my boot heels to be wanderin'
   I'm ready to go anywhere, I'm ready for to fade
   Into my own parade, cast your dancing spell my way
   I promise to go under it

3. Though you might hear laughin', spinnin', wingin' madly across the sun
   It's not aimed at anyone, it's just escapin' on the run
   And but for the sky there are no fences facin'
   And if you hear vague traces of skippin' reels of rhyme
   To your tambourine in time, it's just a ragged clown behind
   I wouldn't pay it any mind,
   It's just a shadow you're seein' that he's chasing

4. Then take me disappearin' through the smoke rings of my mind
   Down the foggy ruins of time, far past the frozen leaves
   The haunted, frightened trees, out to the windy beach
   Far from the twisted reach of crazy sorrow
   Yes, to dance beneath the diamond sky with one hand waving free
   Silhouetted by the sea, circled by the circus sands
   With all memory and fate driven deep beneath the waves
   Let me forget about today until tomorrow

# Positively 4th Street

Registration 4
Rhythm: 8-Beat or Rock

Words and Music by
Bob Dylan

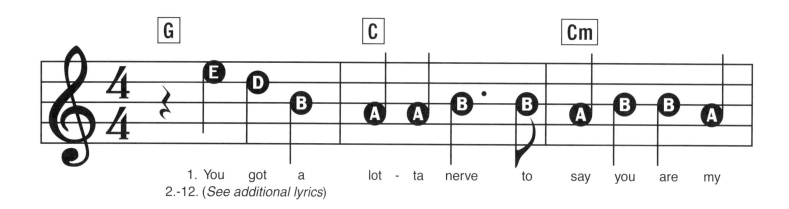

1. You got a lot - ta nerve to say you are my
2.-12. (*See additional lyrics*)

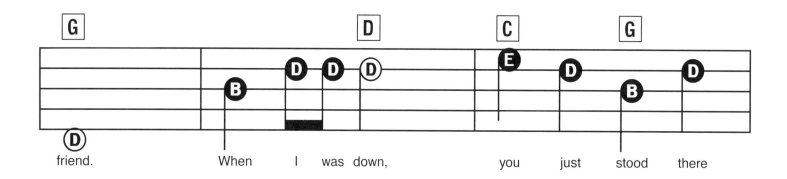

friend. When I was down, you just stood there

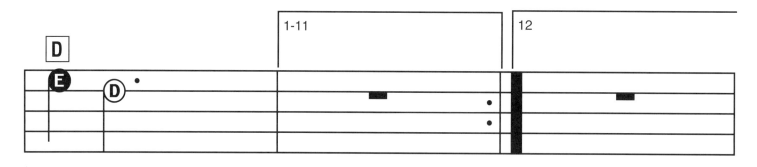

grin - ning.

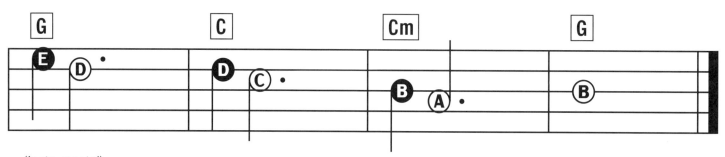

(*Instrumental*)

*Additional Lyrics*

2. You got a lotta nerve
   To say you gotta helping hand to lend.
   You just want to be on
   The side that's winning.

3. You say I let you down.
   You know it's not like that.
   If you're so hurt,
   Why then don't you show it?

4. You say you lost your faith,
   But that's not where it's at.
   You had no faith to lose
   And you know it.

5. I know the reason
   That you talk behind my back.
   I used to be among the crowd
   You're in with.

6. Do you take me for such a fool
   To think I'd make contact
   With the one who tries to hide
   When he don't know to begin with?

7. You see me on the street,
   You always act surprised.
   You say, "How are you?", "Good luck,"
   But you don't mean it.

8. When you know as well as me
   You'd rather see me paralyzed.
   Why don't you just come out once
   And scream it?

9. No, I do not feel that good
   When I see the heartbreaks you embrace.
   If I was a master thief,
   Perhaps I'd rob them.

10. And now I know you're dissatisfied
    With your position and your place.
    Don't you understand
    It's not my problem?

11. I wish that for just one time
    You could stand inside my shoes
    And just for that one moment
    I could be you.

12. Yes, I wish that for just one time
    You could stand inside my shoes.
    You'd know what a drag it is
    To see you.

# Rainy Day Women #12 & 35

Registration 4
Rhythm: Slow Rock or Rock

Words and Music by
Bob Dylan

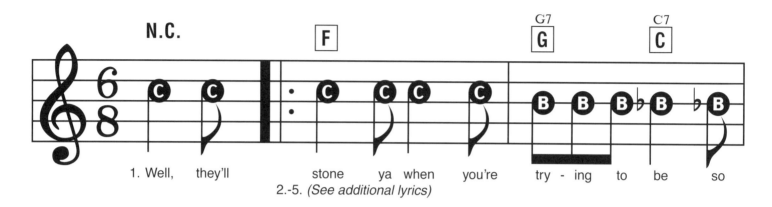

1. Well, they'll stone ya when you're try - ing to be so
2.-5. *(See additional lyrics)*

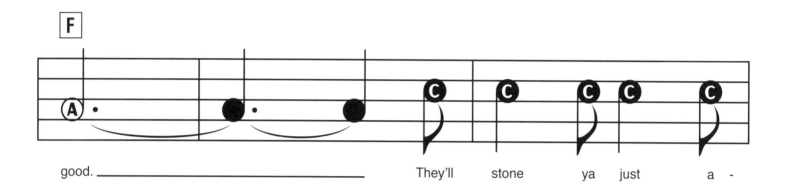

good. _____ They'll stone ya just a -

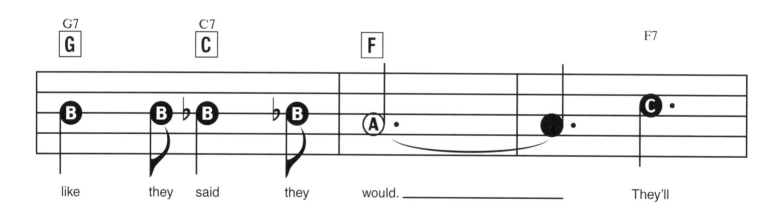

like they said they would. _____ They'll

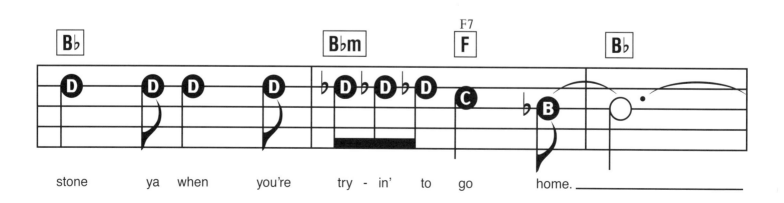

stone ya when you're try - in' to go home. _____

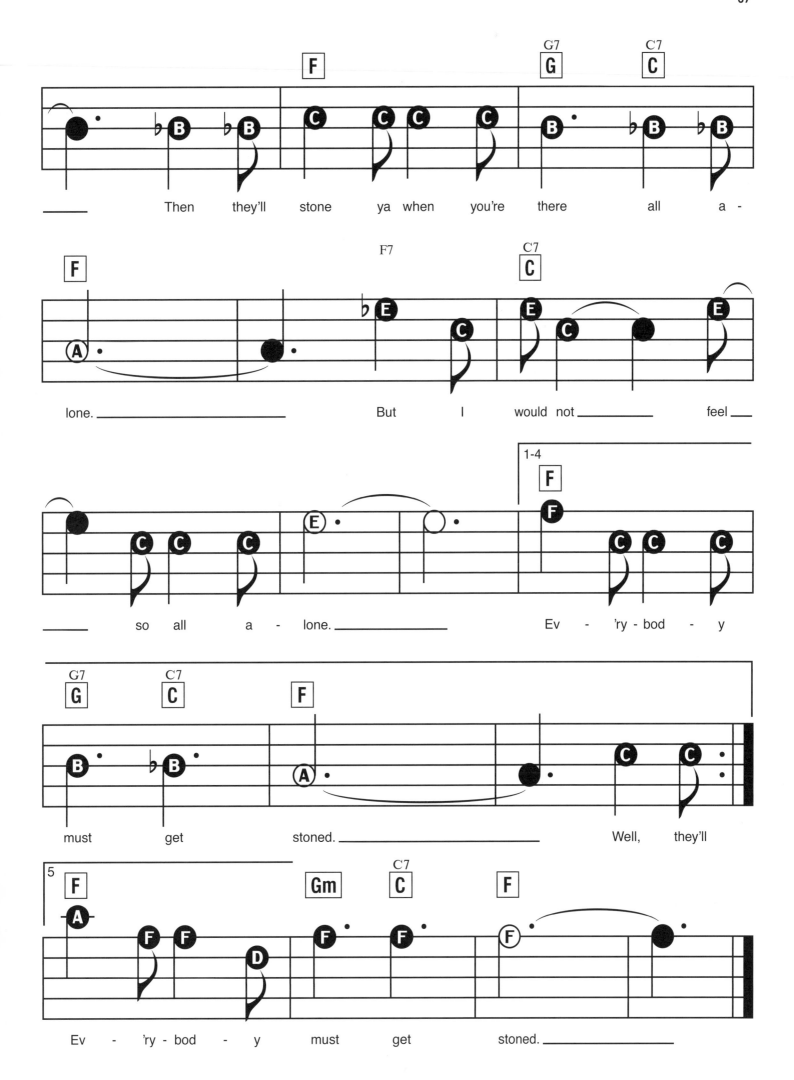

*Additional Lyrics*

2. Well, they'll stone ya when you're walkin' 'long the street.
   They'll stone ya when you're tryin' to keep your seat.
   They'll stone ya when you're walkin' on the floor.
   They'll stone ya when you're walkin' to the door.
   But I would not feel so all alone.
   Everybody must get stoned.

3. They'll stone ya when you're at the breakfast table.
   They'll stone ya when you are young and able.
   They'll stone ya when you're tryin' to make a buck.
   They'll stone ya and then they'll say, "Good luck."
   Tell ya what, I would not feel so all alone.
   Everybody must get stoned.

4. Well, they'll stone you and say that it's the end.
   Then they'll stone you and then they'll come back again.
   They'll stone ya when you're ridin' in your car.
   They'll stone ya when you're playin' playing your guitar.
   Yes, but I would not feel so all alone.
   Everybody must get stoned.

5. Well, they'll stone ya when you walk all alone.
   They'll stone ya when you are walking home.
   They'll stone you and then say you are brave.
   They'll stone you when you are set down in your grave.
   But I would not feel so all alone.
   Everybody must get stoned.

# Shelter from the Storm

Registration 2
Rhythm: 8-Beat or Rock

Words and Music by
Bob Dylan

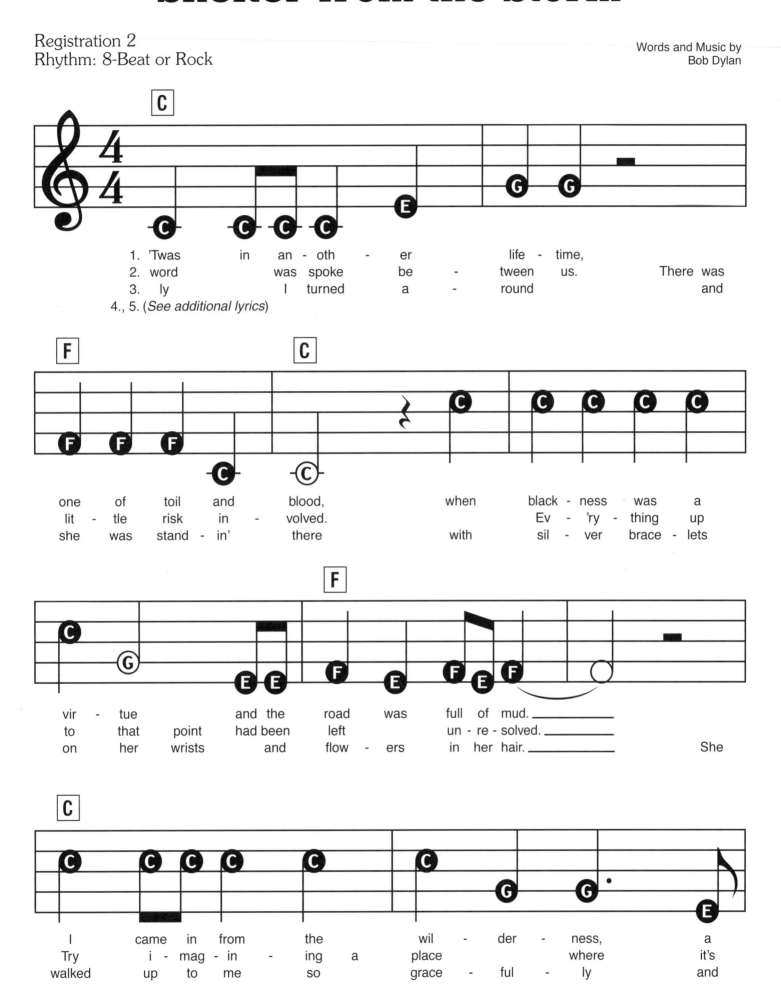

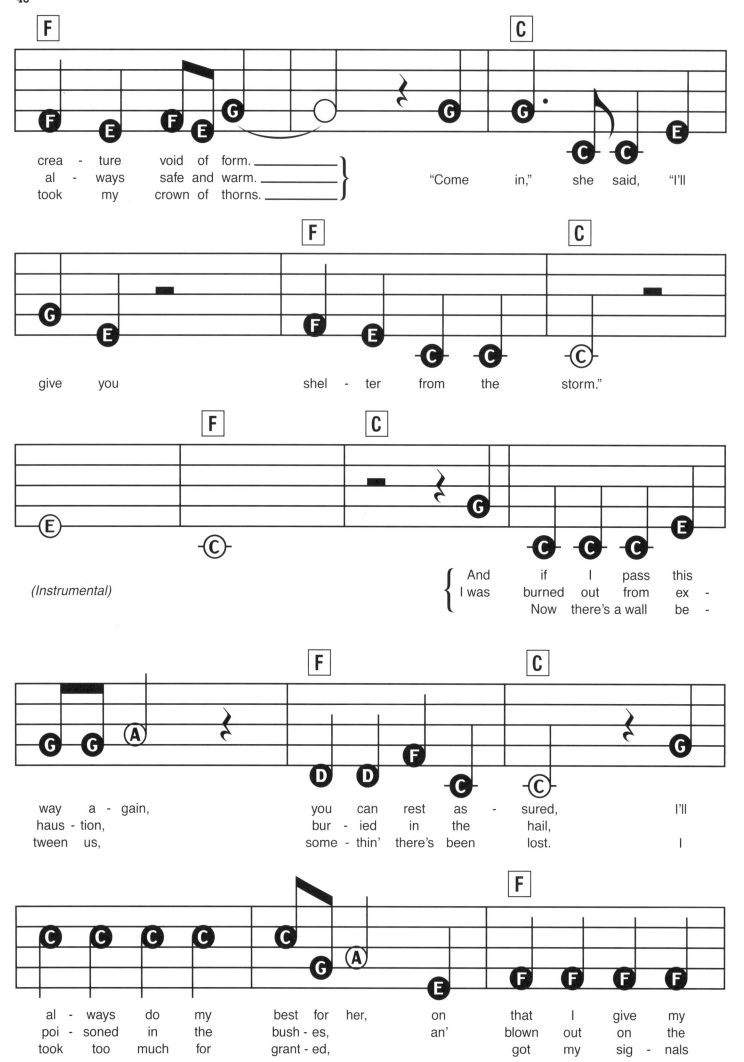

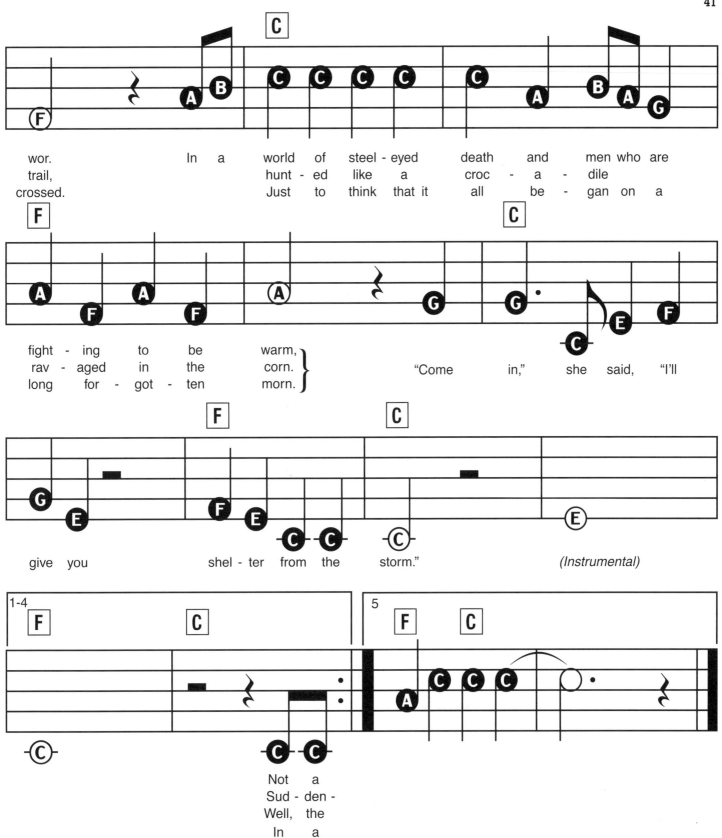

wor.
In a world of steel - eyed death and men who are

trail,
hunt - ed like a croc - a - dile

crossed.
Just to think that it all be - gan on a

fight - ing to be warm,
rav - aged in the corn.
long for - got - ten morn.

"Come in," she said, "I'll

give you
shel - ter from the storm."

*(Instrumental)*

Not a
Sud - den -
Well, the
In a

*Additional Lyrics*

4. Well, the deputy walks on hard nails
    and the preacher rides a mount.
   But nothing really matters much, it's doom alone that counts.
   And the one-eyed undertaker, he blows a futile horn.
   "Come in," she said, "I'll give you shelter from the storm."

   I've heard newborn babies wailin' like a mournin' dove
   And old man with broken teeth stranded without love.
   Do I understand your question, man, is it hopeless and forlorn?
   "Come in," she said, "I'll give you shelter from the storm."

5. In a little hilltop village, they gambled for my clothes.
   I bargained for salvation an' they gave me a lethal dose.
   I offered up my innocence and got repaid with scorn.
   "Come in," she said, "I'll give you shelter from the storm."

   Well, I'm livin' in a foreign country, but I'm bound to cross the line.
   Beauty walks a razor's edge, someday I'll make it mine.
   If I could only turn back the clock to when God and her were born.
   "Come in," she said, "I'll give you shelter from the storm."

# Tangled Up in Blue

Registration 4
Rhythm: 8-Beat or Rock

Words and Music by
Bob Dylan

43

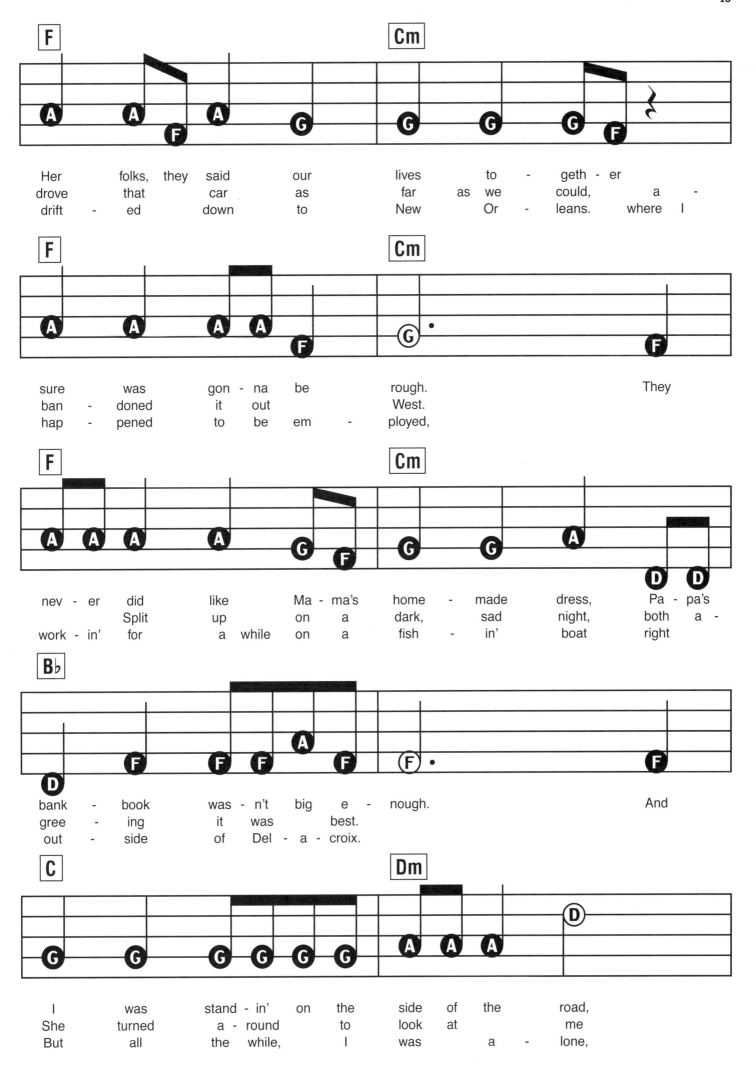

44

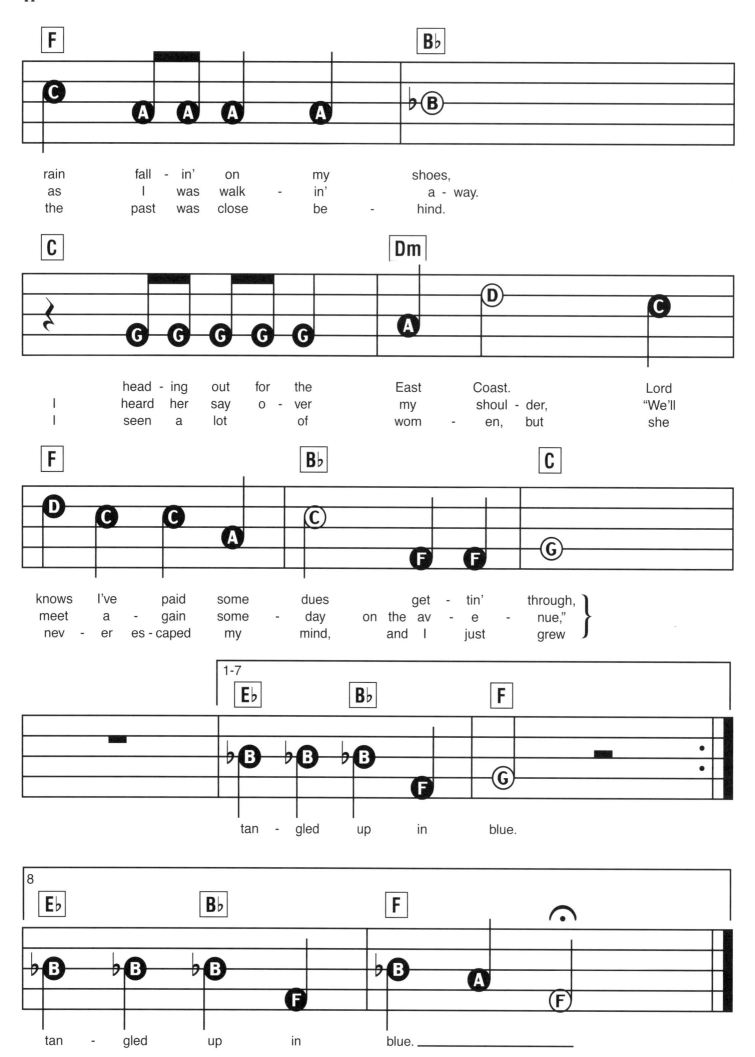

Additional Lyrics

45

*Additional Lyrics*

4. She was workin' in topless place
   And I stopped in for a beer.
   I just kept lookin' at the side of her face
   In the spotlight so clear.
   And later on as the crowd thinned out
   I's just about to do the same.
   She was standing there in back of my chair,
   Said to me, "Don't I know your name?"
   I muttered something underneath my breath.
   She studied the lines on my face.
   I must admit I felt a little uneasy
   When she bent down to tie the laces of my shoe,
   Tangled up in blue.


5. She lit a burner on the stove
   And offered me a pipe.
   "I thought you'd never say hello," she said.
   "You look like the silent type."
   Then she opened up a book of poems
   And handed it to me,
   Written by an Italian poet
   From the thirteenth century.
   And every one of them words rang true
   And glowed like burnin' coal,
   Pourin' off of every page
   Like it was written in my soul from me to you,
   Tangled up in blue.


6. I lived with them on Montague Street
   In a basement down the stairs.
   There was music in the cafés at night
   And revolution in the air.
   Then he started into dealing with slaves
   And something inside of him died.
   She had to sell everything she owned
   And froze up inside.
   And when finally the bottom finally fell out
   I became withdrawn.
   The only thing I knew how to do
   Was to keep on keeping on like a bird that flew
   Tangled up in blue.


   So now I'm goin' back again.
7. I got to get to her somehow.
   All the people we used to know,
   They're an illusion to me now.
   Some are mathematicians,
   Some are carpenter's wives.
   Don't know how it all got started,
   I don't know what they're doin' with their lives.
   But me, I'm still on the road
   Headin' for another joint.
   We always did feel the same,
   We just saw it from a different point of view,
   Tangled up in blue.

# The Times They Are A-Changin'

Registration 8
Rhythm: Waltz

Words and Music by
Bob Dylan

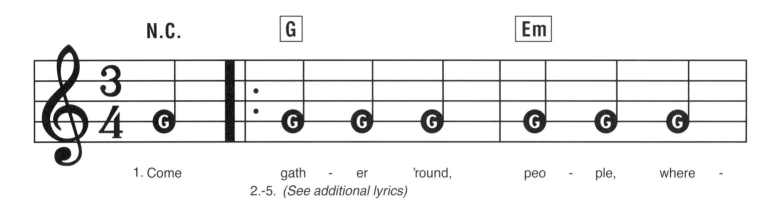

1. Come       gath - er    'round,      peo - ple,      where -
2.-5. *(See additional lyrics)*

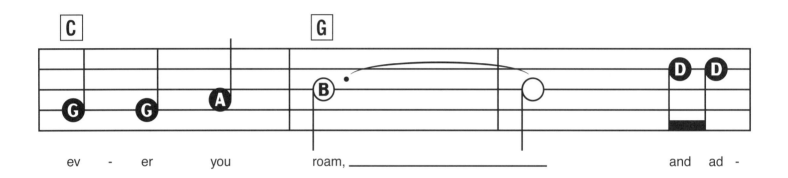

ev - er     you      roam, _____    and ad -

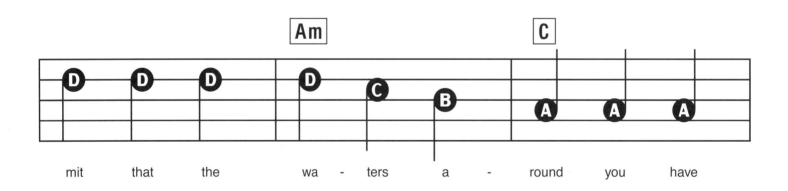

mit     that    the      wa - ters    a - round     you      have

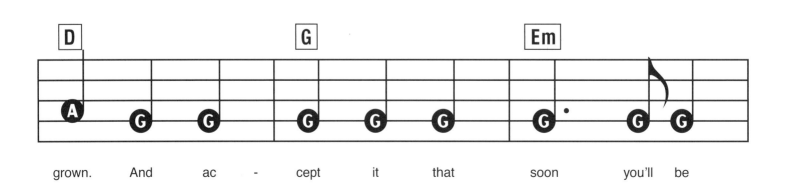

grown.     And     ac - cept     it      that      soon      you'll     be

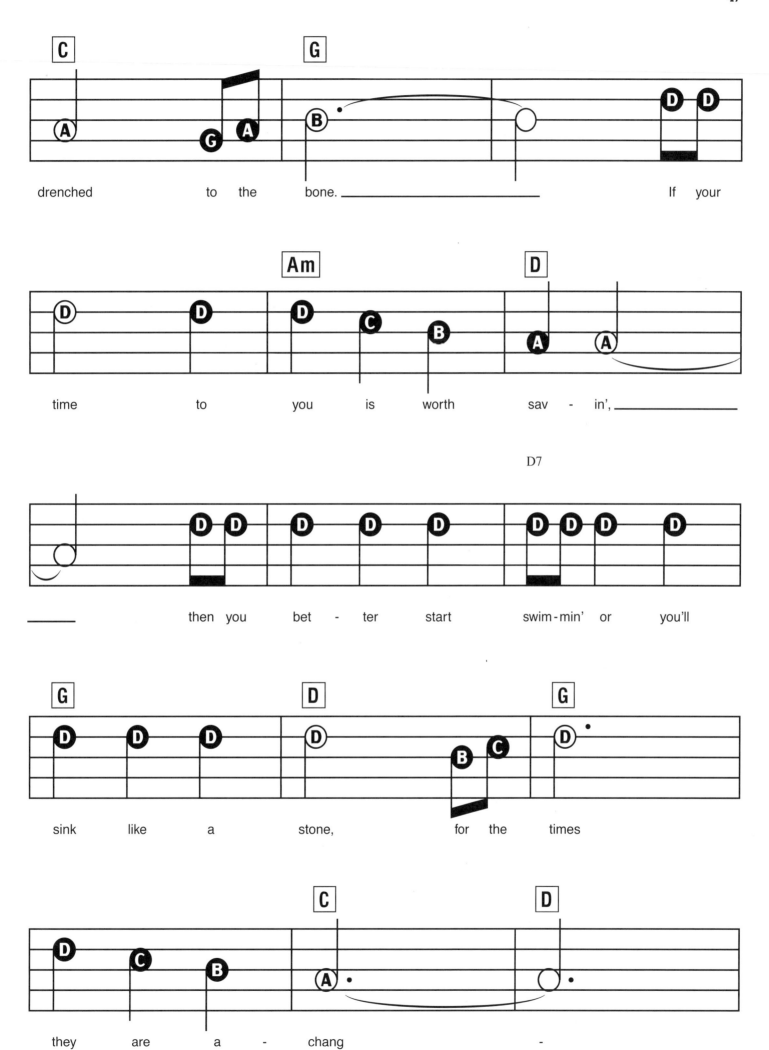

48

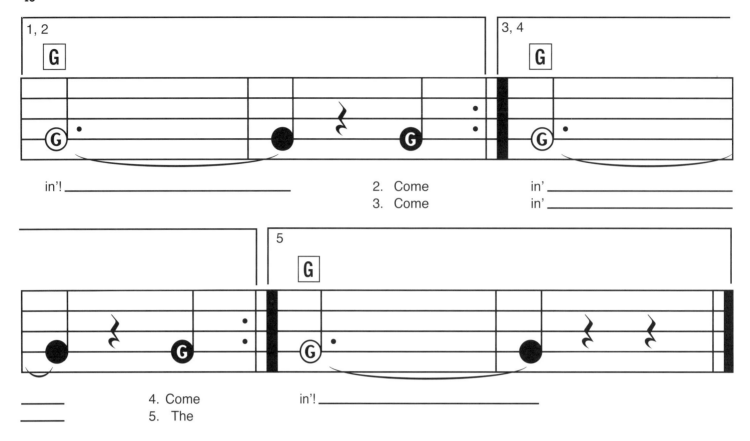

in'! _____  2. Come    in' _____
                              3. Come    in' _____

_____      4. Come    in'! _____
_____      5. The

*Additional Lyrics*

2. Come writers and critics
   Who prophesy with your pen
   And keep your eyes wide
   The chance won't come again.
   And don't speak too soon
   For the wheel's still in spin,
   And there's no tellin' who that it's namin'.
   For the loser now will be later to win,
   For the times they are a-changin'.

3. Come senators, congressmen
   Please heed the call
   Don't stand in the doorway
   Don't block up the hall.
   For he that gets hurt
   Will be he who has stalled,
   There's a battle outside and it's ragin'.
   It'll soon shake your windows and rattle your walls,
   For the times they are a-changin'!

4. Come mothers and fathers
   Throughout the land
   And don't criticize
   What you can't understand.
   Your sons and your daughters
   Are beyond your command,
   Your old road is rapidly agin'.
   Please get out of the new one if you can't lend you hand,
   For the times they are a-changin'.

5. The line it is drawn
   The curse it is cast
   The slow one now will
   Later be fast.
   As the present now
   Will later be past.
   The order is rapidly fadin'.
   And the first one now will later be last,
   For the times they are a-changin'!